Y0-BCW-501

THE HOUSE OF COMMONS AND MONARCHY

By HILAIRE BELLOC

THE FREE PRESS

THE PATH TO ROME

With 80 illustrations by the Author

THE ROMANCE OF TRISTAN AND ISEULT

Translated from the French by J. Bédier

Etc., Etc.

THE HOUSE OF COMMONS AND MONARCHY

By H. BELLOC

LONDON: GEORGE ALLEN & UNWIN LTD.
RUSKIN HOUSE, 40 MUSEUM STREET, W.C. 1

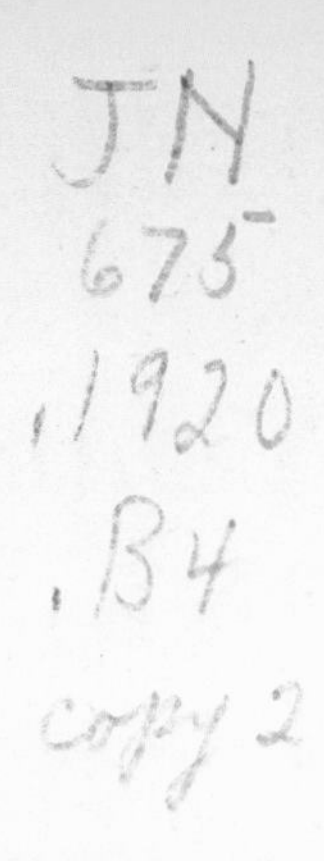

First published in 1920

CONTENTS

twined with the House of Commons as to be almost indistinguishable from it. Through membership of the House of Commons are attained the great prizes of the legal profession, and the very hours and arrangements of the Commons Debates are moulded to the convenience of the Courts.

What great strength such high centralization has given this country in the past, it needs no wide knowledge of history to confirm. Men eager for freedom and dignity of living in the individual rightly demand the separation of the various powers in Sovereignty. They insist on an independent Judiciary; on a Legislature uncontrolled by the Executive. But men who are concerned rather with the strength of the State, and especially with its action abroad, men concerned with the homogeneity and quiet continuance of their country, coupled with its expansion in foreign dominion and its invincibility against foreign aggression, rejoice to recognize a high and successful centralization of Sovereignty, however masked, or under whatever name.

Nowhere has that centralization proceeded to such lengths as it did in the England of the nineteenth century, especially just after the middle of that period. It may be said with justice that the British House of Commons was, in the generation immediately preceding our own, the most absolute and the strongest Prince on earth. That absolute strength was reflected in the peace within, the proud security without, the vast expansion in wealth and territory which this country could boast from the close of the Napoleonic Wars to times well within our own memory.

Such is the fundamental postulate a man must take before proceeding to any examination of our political case to-day. The House of Commons was everything to England. On it all stood—and it worked well.

To-day, as is notorious, it is working badly: and more and more badly. Its authority is failing, or rather has failed; and from that failure chiefly proceeds the political anxiety of our time.

It is my purpose in this essay to examine first why Parliament has failed; next, the cause of this failure being found, to discover what should or may succeed the lost power of the House of Commons.

In this connection two questions have to be answered:

First, whether the organ itself can be healed, i.e., whether the House of Commons can be reformed, or aided in some such fashion as will restore its original position;

Secondly, if this prove impossible, what other organ can take its place.

The thesis I shall maintain is the following:

The House of Commons, though containing a representative element, was, and is, essentially not a representative body, but an Oligarchy; that is, a small body of men segregated from the mass of the citizens and renewing itself. But no Oligarchy works (that is, can be morally accepted or exercise authority) unless it be an Aristocracy. Mere Oligarchy, the mere rule of a clique without the excuse of an imputed excellence, will never be tolerated among men. The whole meaning of Aristocracy is the provision of a sort of worship addressed to the few that govern. Therefore the House of Commons was vigorous and healthy in its function only so long as it was the Aristocratic organ of an Aristocratic State.

For the definition of "The Aristocracy" in an Aristocratic State is, not a body recruited by birth or even from wealth, not a caste (though it may be a caste), least of all a plutocracy, but essentially *an Oligarchy enjoying a Peculiar Respect from its fellow citizens.* Upon the failure of the Aristocratic quality in the House of Commons, upon the decline of that body into a clique no longer respected, its moral authority disappeared; and, with that moral authority disappeared its power of government.

Meanwhile the functions of this highly centralized form of executive, magistracy, and legislature combined, was vastly increased through the rapid development of the modern State. Hence, a double evil and a double peril were present: the rapid accretion of material power in something which, as rapidly, was growing morally unfitted to exercise that power.

In seeking an issue we shall find that no external reform, nor any act from within, can restore an organism so far decayed as is the House of Commons to-day. We shall further find that no subsidiary body, or bodies, such as a Trades Council or other Chambers can take its *sovereign* place. It must be replaced, and can only be replaced in this Great State by that which is the only alternative to aristocracy in a Great State, I mean a Monarchy. If some form of Monarchy does not succeed to the lost inheritance of the House of Commons, the State will lose its greatness.

Such is the argument I set forth to develop.

II

THE HISTORY OF THE NAME "HOUSE OF COMMONS"

IT ORIGINALLY ATTACHED TO SOMETHING QUITE DIFFERENT FROM WHAT WE HAVE KNOWN AS THE HOUSE OF COMMONS FOR THE LAST THREE CENTURIES

II

THE HISTORY OF THE NAME "HOUSE OF COMMONS." IT ORIGINALLY ATTACHED TO SOMETHING QUITE DIFFERENT FROM WHAT WE HAVE KNOWN AS THE HOUSE OF COMMONS DURING THE LAST THREE CENTURIES.

TO understand what has happened to the House of Commons in our time, the nature of its mortal sickness, we must begin with the history of it. First we must learn how it acquired the name it bears; next how that old thing of which it inherited the name disappeared and gave birth to that great *Sovereign* Governing Assembly which has been the Person of England since the Civil Wars.

We say to-day, and with justice, that the House of Commons is, and has been for over two and a half centuries, the capital institution; the centre of the State; an organism gathering up into itself the threads of all the national life, until, to-day—in contrast with all other *modern* States—England is completely centralized, and that centralization lies wholly in this one point: the House of Commons.

But in this definition the modifying words "two and a half centuries" are essential to exactitude. The mere words "House of Commons"—the name—is older by far than the seventeenth century. It is a literal translation of the mediæval phrases "*Communz,*" "*Communitas,*" and the rest; French and Latin titles for certain institutions common to all Christendom in the Middle Ages. But it was in the early seventeenth century that the thing which we call the House of Commons, as distinguished from the name, came into being: say, 1620-50, just as the figment called "The Crown" then first begins to replace the old reality of English Kingship.

There are many patriotic men who would desire that the thing itself should be older, for all patriotic men love to see the institutions of their country derived from as old a lineage as possible. But these should be content with the knowledge that no European nation to-day has a continuous constitutional history of anything like two hundred and fifty years, and that the House of Commons with its three hundred years of continuity is the oldest governing organism in Christendom.

The genesis of this singular, powerful, and national oligarchy was as follows:

When the West arose from its long sleep at the end of the Dark Ages, it broke, as all the world knows, into a new and very vigorous life which we call the life of the Middle Ages.

Europe stood up upon its feet and became a new thing with the Reformation of the Papacy by St. Gregory VII, the imperial adventures of the Normans, and, lastly, the great Crusading march—all matters of the eleventh century. The outward signs of this awakening still remain in all European States, and are the vernacular languages, the Gothic architecture, the codification of custom (and with it of titles), the Universities, the National Kingshops, the Parliaments.

These Parliaments, springing up spontaneously from the body of Christendom, were based, of course, upon the model of the great monastic system, where the representative principle was born. It would be waste of time in so short an essay as this to go into the silly "Teutonic" theories of the last generation, common in the German and

English universities at that time. It was attempted to discover some aboriginal, barbaric, prehistoric origin for a system which obviously and naturally sprang from the conditions of the twelfth and thirteenth centuries. It was like trying to prove a theory that the first, second, and third class on modern railway trains arose from the division of nobles, free men, and serfs six hundred years before our time.

Parliaments were the spontaneous product of that great moment of youth and of spring in our blood, the sunrise or boyhood of which was the twelfth century, and the noon or strong manhood the thirteenth century. It is not germane to this short essay to discuss the doubt as to where the first of these assemblies may have arisen. Nor is it of practical value to history. One might as well discuss where had been found in some county the first green shoots of the year: there was an outburst of new life. Probably the first Parliament arose in that crucible of all our history, the place where the defence of Europe against the Mahommedans was most acute, and where life was therefore most intense —the Southern issues of the Pyrenees. The town of Jaca has a special claim. At any rate the new idea of lay representation modelled on the already long existing monastic system was universal in all the West by the beginning of the thirteenth century, and its effects were equally universal and spontaneous.[1] Communal effort, the modification, aid, restriction, and support of authority from below, was the very spirit of the Middle Ages. That time gave birth, in its passion for reality, to institutions not deduced from abstract formulæ, but corresponding to existing social needs. Therefore these Parliaments (the word means "gatherings for discussion") included the King (or in a Republic the Senate and other chief authorities) and Councils corresponding to the various real divisions of Society. The Council of the most important men, that is, the great Nobles and the Bishops, was permanent, and, with the King, did all the debating and fixing of the laws. But there was also a Council of the mass of Free Men from the towns and villages, and Councils of the lower Clergy. These Councils of Free Men and of Clergy were summoned only for particular occasions. They did no permanent work, as did the Nobles; and all the while the chief Legislator,

[1] The first seeds were sown in this island by King John, who, in 1213, summoned four representatives from each shire to his Council.

still more the chief Executive, was the King.

Now in the case of the Clergy, and in that of the Free Men you had the obvious difficulty that not all of them, even in a small State, could meet in the presence of whatever was the fixed and permanent authority of the State; not all of them, even in a very small State, could crowd into the presence of the King and his Nobles and Bishops. Therefore, following the examples of the great religious orders, was introduced the system of *representation.* The mass of the Clergy and the mass of the Free Men, landholders in the villages, and Burgesses in the towns, chose deputies to speak for them in the Lower Clerical House and the Lower Lay House.

The method of choice was not universal: it differed with local custom and need. The town council or a popular, traditional, gathering directed by the local officer of the King might decide what persons should be sent to the central discussion, so far as laymen were concerned. The clerical elections, as the Church was universally organized, would normally be more regular. But whatever the methods of election the *object* was simple and everywhere the same. The masses, whether clergy or laymen, were *represented*

—just as monks and monastic houses were represented in their central councils—because it was the only way of getting a few to speak for all. *And what they were sent to speak about was taxation.*

On rare occasions, this expanded Council when summoned, finding itself in the presence of the Government, would talk of other things than taxation. If the State was in peril, for instance, the representatives might counsel a remedy. But taxation was the main object of their coming. For the twin conceptions of private property and of liberty were, in the Middle Ages, so strong that our modern idea (which is the old Roman idea) of a tax being imposed arbitrarily by the Government, and being paid without question, was abhorrent to those times. A tax was, for the men of the Middle Ages, essentially a *grant*. The Government had to go to its subjects and say: "We need for public purposes so much: can you meet us? What can you voluntarily give us?" And the essential principle of the Representative Houses of the Clergy and of the Laymen all over Europe was a convocation for this purpose; taxation was in those distant days a *voluntary* subsidy to the needs of the King, that is, of the public service.

It was clear that, such a system once established, the growth of the modern State, with its increasing expenditure and the decay of the King's old feudal revenues, would tend to make the presence of representatives to discuss such voluntary grants more and more a permanent feature of the King's Court and Council. It became a regularly recurrent feature of that Council. With the regular return of representatives to the National Council it at last became necessary that all the "Estates of the Realm" should agree, before any innovation could be introduced as a permanent and binding law, and that they should concur in its promulgation. Thus, for the second period of the Middle Ages, was government conceived throughout a united Christendom.

But with the last century of the Middle Ages there entered into England a feature destined slightly to modify the development of Parliaments *here*. The realm was small, compact, and wealthy, and its Kings had therefore always been at issue with the powerful men below them. The descendants of the great Roman landowners—those whom to-day we call "squires"—were not counterbalanced by the populace in England as they could be in larger countries. There was no room for the King's curbing the rich by relying on the masses, as he did elsewhere —notably in France. There was always a tendency on the part of the English rich territorial lords and of the great merchants in the English towns to encroach upon the power of the King, to act as the spokesmen of the national traditions, and as the masters of the common people.

That tendency might have been checked and might have disappeared, but for a very important revolution in English affairs. This revolution was the usurpation of the Crown by the House of Lancaster in 1399.

By all the ideas of that time this usurpation was a breach in custom and right, and a wound inflicted upon the national life.

Though the usurper was the King's own cousin and the next heir to the throne, he had to do what all men have to do when they are in the wrong before the public: he had to find allies who would, at a price, support an action which they did not morally approve, and to which their souls were alien. The Lancastrian usurpation during its little moment of power (less than the lifetime of a man) tried all the tricks which the history of usurpers has made familiar. It tried terrorism by violent punishments. It tried foreign adventure. Above all, it relied upon an artificial alliance with, and deference to, the wealthier class, lay and cleric. The growing power of the squires and the big merchants of the towns was bribed—insecurely—to the Lancastrian side.

The squires were given more power by the King. He truckled to them and to the merchant fortunes. The rich men were made *local magistrates*—a policy fatal to equality, and, therefore, in the long run, to kingship—they began to dominate local life; they captured representation. The faint beginnings of aristocratic rule had appeared through the Lancastrian tradition, even before the Reformation approached.

The storm of the Reformation, therefore, the effects of which are the turning point of the whole history of Europe, fell upon an England in which the representative body, the Estates of the Realm, the Parliament, was already beginning to be an oligarchy, and in which the Lower House had already become permanently a House of Squires and Merchants. In such a state was the general European institution of the "Parliament" in England, in such a state were the "Commons," when the wind of the Reformation blew first upon this island.

This was four centuries ago, and at that time your local representative who was sent to the Commons, though now sent regularly, was still in the main no more than a person sent to grant taxation for his class. Such men rarely debated important affairs of State (save in a great crisis). They had very little to do with the initiation of new laws, and hardly anything to do with policy. They were utterly different from what we call the House of Commons in later times.

When, as an effect of the Reformation, the squires and merchants had become the governing power of the realm ; when England, after the century of the Reformation, had become an oligarchy ; when the King's power had disappeared—the House of Commons was to become above all *an expression of the governing class*, and to assume that modern formation, to become that modern *thing* which we know, and which has been associated with all the glory and strength of England for three hundred years.